STEPHEN LEHNER AND LA...

THE COMPLEAT BUSINESSMAN

ANGUS
& ROBERTSON
PUBLISHERS

*Take your secretary
into your confidence*

Entertain on weekends

*Don't get involved
in office politics*

*Don't come back
without the order*

*Permit grievances
to be aired freely*

*Know your
competition's weak spot*

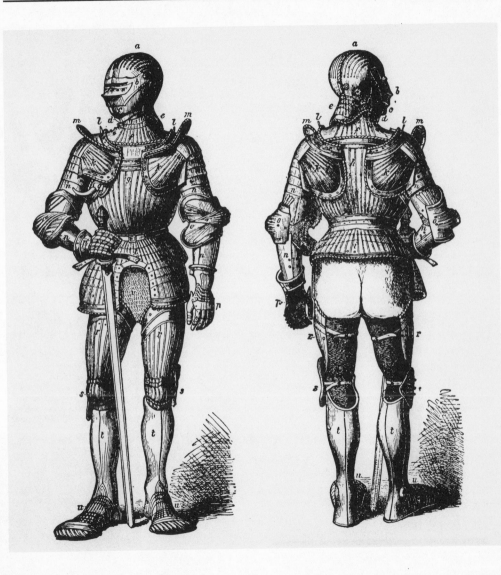

*Use your expense
account wisely*

*Give every
job applicant a
personal interview*

Find a relaxing hobby

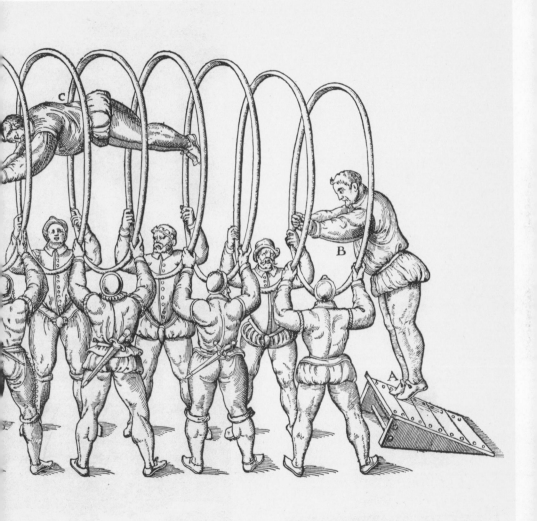

*Don't promise more
than you can deliver*

*Hold staff
meetings regularly*

*Participate in
community activities*

*Fit the man
to the job*

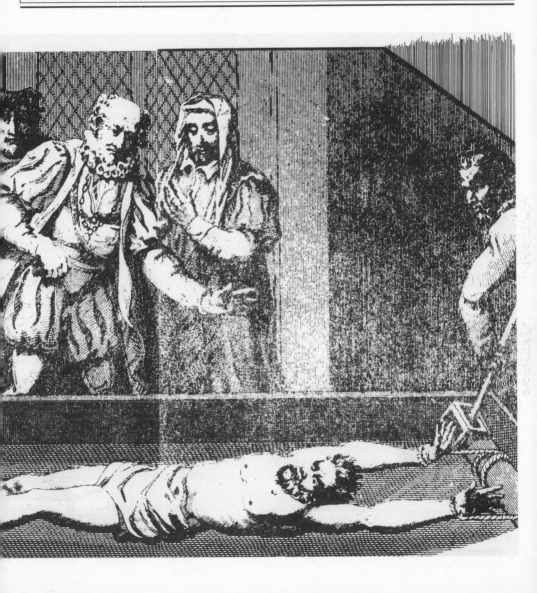

*Try to settle
differences out of court*

*Give the customer
more than he expects*

*Ask for a
raise gracefully*

Find a relaxing hobby

*Don't underestimate
the importance of a
good receptionist*

*Emphasise the danger
of industrial accidents*

*Make sure
first-class executives
travel first class*

*Dramatise your
sales presentations*

Develop a comprehensive
junior executive
training program

*Don't hold
conferences after lunch*

Don't win the argument . . .
and lose the sale

Keep sales talks brief.

*Don't let the coffee break
get out of hand*

Find a relaxing hobby

*Don't overdo
those three hour lunches*

*Be properly prepared
for board meetings*

*Develop your
own methods for
handling competitors*

*Hold meetings at the
home office regularly*

*Investigate the
possibilities of automation*

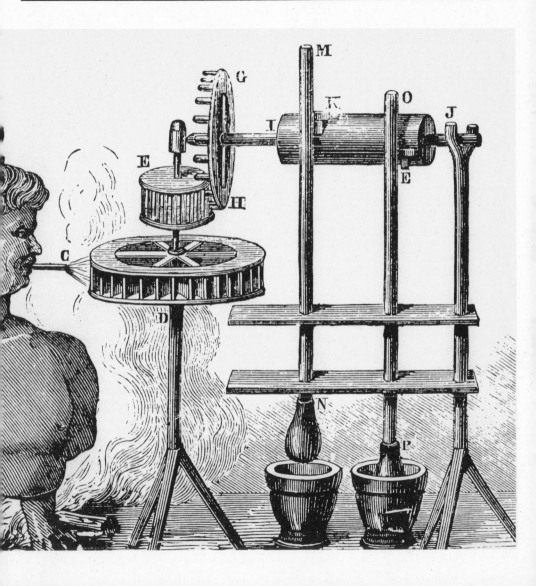

*Free key personnel
from routine work*

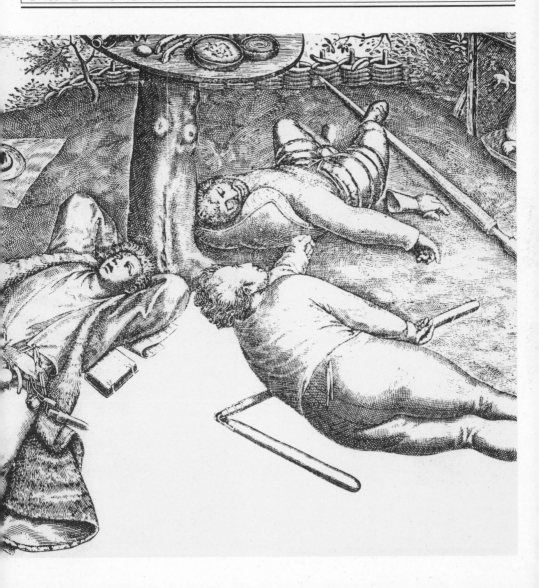

Hire a secretary
who doesn't panic

*Don't discuss business
at company picnics*

Plan sales campaigns carefully before opening new territories

*Don't spread
yourself too thin*

*Let your staff
know there's room
at the top*

Fight for a private office

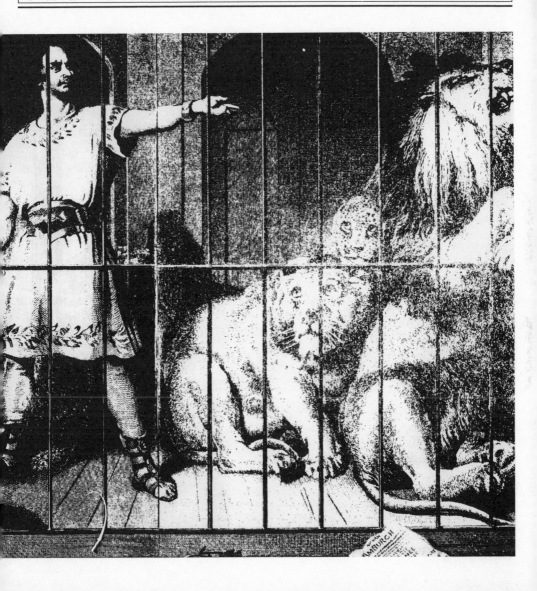

*Make sure
your secretary can
handle emergencies*

*Show a
personal interest
in employees' problems*

*Don't have
more than three martinis
for lunch*

Find a relaxing hobby

ANGUS & ROBERTSON PUBLISHERS

Unit 4, Eden Park, 31 Waterloo Road,
North Ryde, NSW, Australia 2113, and
16 Golden Square, London W1R 4BN,
United Kingdom

Originally published in the
United States of America
by Price/Stern/Sloan
Publishers, Inc., Los Angeles, California
First published in Australia
by Angus & Robertson Publishers in 1987
First published in the United Kingdom
by Angus & Robertson (UK) in 1987

National Library of Australia
Cataloguing-in-publication data

Lehner, Stephen.
   The compleat businessman.

   ISBN 0 207 15533 X.

   1. Businessmen — Anecdotes, facetiae, satire, etc. I.
   Sloan, Lawrence. II. Title.

808.87'9352338

Printed in Australia by the Globe Press Pty Ltd